W9-AHM-355

Take Comfort, Too

More Reflections of Hope
for Family Caregivers

By Denise M. Brown

Thank you for buying our book!

© 2010 Tad Publishing and Consulting Co. and Denise M. Brown

All rights reserved. No part of this book may be reproduced or transmitted in any form or by any means, electronic or mechanical, including photocopying, recording, or by any information storage and retrieval system, without permission in writing from the publisher.

Published by Tad Publishing and Consulting Co., Park Ridge, IL.

ISBN 978-0-557-97349-1

For information and support as you care for your family members, please visit Caregiving.com.

To my siblings (Marianne, Keith, Tim and Julie): Thank you for all of your support and love.

Take Comfort, Too

More Reflections of Hope for Family Caregivers

Table of Contents

~ **Spring** ~

"Expect to have hope rekindled. Expect
your prayers to be answered in
wondrous ways. The dry seasons in life
do not last. The spring rains
will come again."
~ Sarah Ban Breathnach

Down

No matter what you do, there will be days
when you're down. You feel sad,
disillusioned, tired. And, no kind word, no
loving hug and no inspirational saying can
pick you up.

You're just down.

And, that's okay. Sometimes, you need to be
down to lick your wounds, catch your
breath, wipe your tears.

You'll be down. But, know that there's
always an upswing on its way. And, having
felt the pain of being down, you'll savor the
joy of being up.

Embrace

Caregiving can seem to engulf your entire life, so much so that it becomes your life. Without your knowledge or even your approval, it can add blinders, causing you to see yourself as only caregiver, not the individual you once were.

Your life prior to caregiving may not be the same within your life of caregiving, but you can blend bits and pieces of that past within your present. You are an individual with interests, opinions, gifts, wisdom, talents and blessings.

Embrace these. Carry them with you. Grow them.

Embrace them.

Captivate

It seems the caregiving has captured your life. This week, consider what captivates your soul?

Giving pause to consider what makes you breathe, especially when a life event makes it so hard to breathe, is just as important as doctor visits, medication reminders, and grab bars in the bathtub. To keep you from losing yourself to the caregiving, take time to ponder your soul. What brings it to live?

A lively soul means a well-lived life.

Kind

Although you may try not to, some days you may think: What kind of life is this?
It's not the kind of life you envisioned for your caree, for yourself, for others in your life affected by caregiving. And, that kind of life can steal your kindness, replacing it with resentment and bitterness.

Know this.

You have a kind of life that builds on your values and your priorities. You have the kind of life that focuses on relationships and works off compromises.

You have the kind of life that has good and bad. And, that's okay. You have a life with a little bit of bitterness that's outweighed by your kindness.

Your kind of life is all about the grace of living.

Over

Sometimes, it's the word you dread to hear. When a relationship ends, you may hear, "It's over." When a wonderful experience ends, you think, "It's over." You may clench your teeth when you're told to "get over it."

And, sometimes, you feel that the life you want is over there, rather than right here. When you lengthen the word, you see its power. You overcome: Difficult days, gut-wrenching challenges, overwhelming obstacle.

Every time you overcome, you become. You become exactly who you were meant to be: Strong, wise, gracious.

In the over comes the being.

Change

In a caregiving role, change means something kinda awful. Your caree has a change in condition, which impacts both of you in really sad and difficult ways. Your family changes because of the caregiving experience, which leaves you feeling lonely and alone. You change because of caregiving, perhaps becoming someone you no longer recognize (and, sometimes, like).

So it's understandable that you may view "change" as a four-letter word.

You do have positive changes in your life. Your idea of friendships and family has changed which means you have deeper relationships than before. Your ability to manage a crisis has changed so much that you barely bat an eye at the upsets that once ruined your day.

Your understanding of your own inner strength means you face new challenges with a knowledge that you can rather than with a fear that you can't.

Life has changed. You have changed. Accept the bad changes and embrace the good.

Hunger

When you're hungry for food, you feel the emptiness in your stomach.

In caregiving, when you're hungry, you feel a longing in your soul.

In caregiving, you may crave freedom, a reprieve, a lucky break, a grateful smile, a loving hand. You crave because you seem rarely to receive.

When you feel such emptiness, you may feel the need to feed the hunger with Snickers, Doritos and Diet Coke. But those three will only leave you hungrier.

When your soul cries for nourishment, turn to the support and resources that honor you and your caregiving role. Your faith, your friends, your support community have the food to feed your hunger. We understand your choices and your values.

We understand. Feed off us.

Tempting

In caregiving, it's tempting to close your eyes. When you close your eyes, you don't have to see the problems, the decline, the shambles that caregiving can create.

It's tempting to assume that, in closing your eyes, it all disappears. If you can't see it, then it must not exist. It's also tempting to believe it's too much for you to handle. So, you close your eyes because you feel you are too weak to see.

Close your eyes–but only for sleep. You can keep your eyes open. You have the strength, wisdom and resources to look around and see the facts of caregiving. You can see and you can act. You can manage the problems, you can handle the declines, you can create order out of shambles. And, when you feel you can't, reach out to those who can support you.

When temptation comes, choose to keep your eyes open. You can.

Peace of Mind

Insurance companies promise you can purchase peace of mind from them.

Buy your insurance for your home and car. But, save your money for the peace of mind.

Here's why:

Peace of mind comes from acceptance of time.

When we accept this time in our life, no matter how discouraging this time may be, we give ourselves peace of mind. When we accept our caree's time in this life, that his or her time is on time, we give ourselves peace of mind. When we accept the passing of time as natural and not as the enemy, we give ourselves peace of mind.

When we accept, we lay down the sword, we end the war waging inside.

Peace comes from acceptance.

Pound

In your caregiving role, you pound the pavement looking for help and resources. And, in your role, your heart pounds regularly—with fear, anxiety, worry and guilt.

Keep pounding the pavement. Take breaks when you feel the resources and help seem elusive. But, keep going.

And, when your heart pounds (and your hands sweat), think about pounding the pavement for comfort. Who can help settle your heart? A pounding heart deserves a calming presence—your journal, support group, a friend, your therapist or coach.

In caregiving, you'll face pounds of pavement and feel pounds of heart beats.

Pound them out, knowing a lonely journey like caregiving is never meant to be spent alone. You have support to encourage your search for help and to comfort your heartache.

Choice

You may feel that you have no choice about the events that have shaped your life today.

You do have a choice: You can choose how you would like to handle these very events. You can choose to approach relationships, situations and experiences as those that teach you, even comfort you, often bringing about opportunities you never dreamed possible.

Your choice is in what you do what with your life becomes.

Some believe that you repeat the experiences of your past until you learn the lessons that you need for your future.

Choose today to learn the lessons that you need for tomorrow.

Green

We're all looking to live a lifestyle that's green, one that's good for the world and for our future.

You can go green, too.

Go green to use your energy wisely— focusing on relationships, activities, and responsibilities that honor you.

Go green by respecting your environment— clearing clutter, believing in yourself, inspiring others.

Go green by re-fueling with healthy options —choosing a diet and exercise program that invigorates and protects.

Go green by nurturing your body and soul— using movement, thoughts, and words to reflect your best.

Go green!

Red

Some days, you're going to see red.

The help is late. So, you see red. A supportive family member seems unusually uncooperative. So, you see red. A service provider bails on an agreement. So, you see red.

Rather than see red, wear it.

When a service provider seems to take advantage of you, put on your red and say: "I'm upset right now. We had an agreement and this wasn't it. I'm only honoring our original agreement."

When you and a family member butt heads, put on your red and say: "We're having a tough day today. Let's talk about this tomorrow when we have cooler heads."

When the help arrives late, put on your red and say: "You're late today. I expect you to be on time. When you're on time, then I'm on time. When you're late, then I'm late. What will you adjust so you can be here on time?"

Today, how will you put on your red?

Pit

We may have many pits.

We may sometimes say about circumstances and situations: This is the pits.

We may sometimes think about our life, as it is right now: This is the pits.

We feel a pit in the bottom of our stomach when we feel dread or fear.

But, there's another side to pits. They became a great title to a book ("If Life is a Bowl of Cherries, What Am I Doing in the Pits?" by Erma Bombeck). And, we have a beautiful Pitt (Brad) to watch on the big screen. And, pits and their hard shells protect the seeds (which create new growth) in fruits and vegetables.

Life can sometimes be the pits. When it feels awful, use your pit, your strengths which become your hard shell. Your strengths may be your tenacity, your sense of humor, your pragmatic viewpoint. Under your strengths lies your new growth, your new opportunities. And, those opportunities will be as fun as watching Brad on the big screen.

Dry

Are you caught in a flood?

Your flood may be too much to do and too little time to do it.

So, how do you keep dry?

Keep in mind:

1. Set priorities. What's important to you? What are the most pressing events, relationships and responsibilities? Your priorities take preference.

2. Say "no." You honor every request made to you, even those to which you say "no." You honor them by being honest about your ability to take them on. If you can't, say "no." It's okay.

3. Stick to your limits. When does your day end? 8 p.m.? Then, a request from a friend for a phone call at 9 p.m. is past your bedtime. Schedule it at another time. When do you provide personal care to your caree? Then, that time is off limits to anything but that. How much can you handle? As much as you can. When you've reached your limit, respect it.

Set, say, stick. Three steps to staying dry.

Tax

What's taxing for you?

The worry? The unrelenting work? The constant needs? The piles of recently-laundered clothes in need of a home? The casserole dishes crying for a home-cooked meal? The dust bunnies bouncing about your slippers? Or, is is just getting your taxes done that you find taxing?

When you have the responsibility for the health care needs of another, everything else can seem like an insurmountable tasks, even those as seemingly simple as laundry, cooking and cleaning.

This week, leave the laundry, cooking and cleaning. Focus your attention on what's really important: Moments with a supportive friend who sees how your soul shines, quiet time with your thoughts so you find your perspective, romance with your spouse (or caree) so you give and receive love. The laundry, cooking and cleaning can wait, just for a few days.

Language

When you find yourself in caregiving, you may feel like you've moved to another country. You just don't speak or understand this language.

And, then caregiving ends. Overnight, you wake up in yet another country. It all looks different. It all sounds different. It's another new language.

It's just awful.

When you wake up in a new country, how do you manage?

Manage by keeping the familiar—those who support and love you; that which brings you comfort and peace; thoughts which calm and quiet you.

Learning a new language can be complicated. Sometimes, it's as simple as knowing you will because you already did.

With time, you will speak fluidly the language of life.

ESP

ESP usually means "extrasensory perception." In caregiving, it means: Execute a Special Plan.

When you look around and think, "I'm out of options. I can't find another choice," use your ESP. When you want to sit and cry because nothing seems to work, use your ESP. When you want to run and hide because it seems so much bigger than you, use your ESP.

Your ESP contains ideas, suggestions, support and inspirations. Turn a box or a folder into your ESP that includes:
- the good ideas you hear and read;
- a directory of phone numbers for organizations and individuals who may be able to help;
- pages from books that offer tips on making difficult decisions;
- past ESPs, including what part of the plan worked and why it worked;
- photos and quotes that bring comfort.

Then, when you feel caregiving spinning out of control, go to your ESP. Your ESP does just that—helping you execute a very special plan when a very special plan is exactly what's needed.

Dream

We dream at night.

Why can't we also dream during the day?

Why can't we dream of the life we want?
Why bother, you may say, my dreams will
never come true. They can't come true
during caregiving.

Maybe. And, maybe not. Dream:

- You stand your ground with grace
  and self-respect with those who
  would like to undercut your efforts;
- You see and embrace the moments of
  joy present each day for you;
- You live a life that reflects your
  values;
- You continue to enjoy those
  activities and hobbies that lighten
  your step;
- You look back at your life and can
  say: I'm so glad I did that;
- You evaluate your needs and then
  take steps to have them met;
- You look back at your life and can
  say: I'm so glad I said that;
- You have a bank account that allows
  you to make your choices;
- You consider your wants and then go
  out and get them;
- You have relationships which you
  love and which love you right back;

- You look good when you walk into a room (any room).

You have so much to dream about. Close your eyes. Dream.

Music

Music seems quite miraculous.

Often, our memories can be tied to a song. We hear a certain song and we're transformed to another decade, a different life, a younger self.

When we hear a snappy tune, we tap our feet, sway our head, snap our fingers. And, singing a favorite song feels like the best kind of scream.

We also can make music without having to carry a tune. The right relationship, in which we just fit, can be like a beautiful melody. The exchange of a smile between you and a treasured someone can be like a perfect harmony.

And, when you write about your caregiving journey in your journal (or on your blog), you write the lyrics to a very special ballad. It's a little bit of a concert symphony, a little bit of a musical and a lot of dramatic opera.

Most important, it's your song. Sing the song and dance the music. Flow to the sound of caregiving. And, in the flow, find the energy to face tomorrow.

Tomorrow

We hope that our tomorrows will be bright and giving and fulfilling.

Sometimes, those tomorrows, the tomorrows we hope for, can seem years away. And, that can make it hard to look forward to the true tomorrow, the day after today.

In caregiving, the chance that tomorrow will bring heartache, or finality, or yet another challenge is part of every day.

And, in that knowledge, lies the blessing.

You live for today. You do your best to resolve conflicts now so they don't weigh down your spirit. You speak your truths because, well, why wait? You embrace your potential and act on the opportunities. You learn what you can—about your caree, the disease process, yourself. You live in peace.

Tomorrow may hold pain. How you live today means you can hold the pain of any day right next to its promise.

Spring

The miracle of spring is nature's greenness.

Seemingly overnight, tree's empty branches become lush playground for leafs. The leaves' handiwork seems miraculous. The work done in winter and the endurance of rain storms led to the buds, which became the blooms.

The days of caregiving can feel like days of winter and then rain. You feel cold from the daily grind, the on-going losses, the loneliness. You feel worn out from the tears--of anger, sadness, frustration.

Know that the winter and then the rain of caregiving will become the beauty of your new growth. Your spring will sprout in ways worthy of a rainbow.

Food

When a fridge is full with food, a house feels rich. When it's empty, the house feels poor.

Are you full of the food which helps you feel your life's riches?

Food which can help you feel full includes:
- Friendships which support;
- Quiet time which calms;
- Touch which gives love;
- Activities which invigorate;
- Habits which promote health;
- Relationships which comfort;
- Goals which challenge.

When you feel your life's fridge is empty, consider what you need: A friend, a quiet time, a touch, an activity, a habit, a relationship or a goal. Then, get it or do it.

Nourish your life with great food; it will feed your soul.

Pace

During a crash in a car race, a pace car appears, keeping racers safe by keeping them at the same, slower, speed.

At certain times in life, we all need a pace car, a reminder to take it slow.

We may need to take it slow during life's lows in order to avoid snap decisions or rushed judgments or harsh words.

We may need to take it slow during life's highs in order to create memories and express gratitude and savor the moment.

We can be our own pace car. We can tell ourselves to slow, to take a deep breath, to be silent. For a moment, we can just be.

When we are our own pace car, we can manage the lows and celebrate the highs.

Backstage

Backstage, actors let their hair down after doing their job on the stage.

After you complete your tasks and duties, how do you let your hair down backstage?

Your backstage may be a corner in a room, your journal, your garden. Wherever it is, use your backstage to just be, whether you be sad, tired, disappointed, relieved or hopeful.

Be backstage at some point during your day. It removes the jitters of being on stage the rest of your day.

Elevator

Life has its ups and downs. Caregiving, though, can seem like an one-way elevator —it just goes down.

Caregiving can be a downer. You see so much suffering. And, so much seems to suffer because of caregiving: Friendships, relationships, career goals, your health, your independence, your confidence.

Is it possible to go up?

You push the "Up" button on your elevator when:
- You choose forgiveness, especially with yourself.
- You keep the faith.
- You embrace humor.
- You allow mistakes and mis-steps.
- You express gratitude.
- You keep kindness in your words and actions.
- You accept your feelings, in particular, the sadness and grief.

It can seem that we are not in control of our elevator ride. When, really, the controls are within our reach.

Search

Do you feel like life is one big search?

You search for help, answers, treatment options, support, information. And, then, sometimes, you feel like you search for new friends, new jobs, new homes.

Even worse, the search for acceptance, understanding and love can be absolutely exhausting.

Wouldn't it be nice to stop the search and just prop your feet for rest?

This week, rest. Let the search go. In particular, let the search for acceptance, understanding and love go.

Because you are accepted, understood and loved.

The search is over.

Magic

If only, we can sometimes think, we could wave a wand to make all the difficulties of life disappear.

Wouldn't that be magical?

Difficulties uncover blessings. Once uncovered, these blessings manifest into a perspective, a belief and a knowledge that life, because of its imperfections, is perfect.

That's the magic. Embrace the difficulties for they lead to the magical wonders of life-- wonders all deserving of you.

Say It

Regrets. Wouldn't it be wonderful to live a life of minimal regrets?

Often, the regrets are about the "not's", not verbalizing our feelings to those most important in our lives. We may stay silent out of fear, which often gets our tongue (beating out the cat). We may be afraid that our feelings aren't reciprocated. Or, we may be afraid to show emotion. We may be afraid we won't say the right thing.

When it comes from the heart, it's always right. And, it's about the giving, rather than the receiving. Your ability to express yourself is the true gift. Let the words on your lips truly reflect the love in your heart.

Today, say it. Tell family members and friends what they mean to you. Tell your caree how much you've learned from him or her. Be the one who does it, who turns intangible feelings into tangible.

Say it. Because you deserve a life full of love, not regrets.

~ **Summer** ~

"To believe in life is to believe
there will always be someone who will
water the geraniums."
-- Flavia

Breeze

Wouldn't it be nice if Life, and its sisters
and brothers, were a breeze?

Imagine that finding the right job, the best
spouse, the timely caregiving decision is as
gentle of an experience as a summer breeze.

If only.

Maybe Life, and its Twists and Turns, can be
like a breeze. Perhaps we become the
tornado that kicks the breeze into a driving
wind. What if our belief in ourselves and our
abilities calmed the tornado?

You are right. You are best. You are timely.

You are the gentle breeze in Life.

Flower

Before caregiving, perhaps you felt like a flower in bloom.

Then, with caregiving, one by one, a petal gets plucked. The sadness takes one, the frustration takes another, the worry takes another, the guilt takes two.

Now, you feel like a flower with just a few petals, like a flower that's barely survived a horrible storm. How do you become full again?

Fullness comes from new growth. You can grow new petals when you:

- Practice forgiveness, especially of yourself, daily. You are doing your best, which is the absolute best you can do;
- Spend time regularly in quiet reflection, being grateful for your blessings;
- Talk about your difficult moments with a support system that comforts;
- Make your needs a priority in your schedule.

Your new growth will be more beautiful, more powerful and more dazzling than ever.

You'll flower again.

Cabana

We all need a cabana, a place in the sun that protects from the harmful rays, but keeps us in the midst of fun.

Today, visualize your cabana. It could be on the sand in the Caribbean, the South of France, a cruise ship in the Mediterranean. On those days, when you want to run away, but your responsibilities keep you in place, visualize a visit to your cabana. Enjoy relaxing in your lounge chair, sipping cold drinks, listening to the sound of waves hitting the shore, watching the sun glistening off the pristine water.

We all need a cabana, a place in the sun that protects from the harmful rays, but keeps us in the midst of fun.

Give Up

What have you been holding on to that no longer works for you?

We may hang onto relationships, expectations and duties that just don't work any longer. We may hang on out of habit.

Most likely, we hold out of fear. Giving up means making a change. Nothing is scarier than change.

If you give up what no longer works for you, you make room for new possibilities--better relationships, more realistic expectations and more important responsibilities. What you give up means you have potential for greater gains.

Today, what will you give up to better your life?

Empathy

Because you care, you have the ability to feel for your caree; you are empathetic to your caree's pain, mourning, frustration and fear. You feel your caree's longing for a life without an illness or disability, the longing for a life that's full of trips in the car, outings with friends, visits with family members.

Your empathy allows you to provide loving care. But, it also can lead to greater depression, more anxiety and intense anxiety. Feeling for two can be downright awful.

When you tell your story, include the story of your caree's feelings--and how those feelings affect you. Talk about your caree's heartbreaks, longings, fears. And, talk about your sadness and depression. Share this story with an empathetic support system so that these feelings comfort, rather than haunt, you and your caree. Suppressing the emotions increases their intensity and their hold over you and your caree. Sharing them brings the tears that heal.

The ability to be empathetic is wonderful and rare. Protect your ability; express and release the emotions you and your caree experience.

Life

Consider this: Parenting teaches you how to love. Caregiving teaches you how to live.

How are you living your life today to the fullest?

We're never promised another day. How are living today without regrets? How are you nurturing those relationships that nurture you? And, how are you living so that your legacy lives on after you?

Live.

Culture

What's your caregiving culture?

Organizations create a culture so that creativity, problem-solving and teamwork thrive. You can do the same in your caregiving role.

What culture do you want to create about your caregiving role? Which priorities, relationships and goal will your caregiving culture honor? And, which will your culture let go?

Your caregiving culture will reflect your values, your wishes for yourself and for your caree, and your relationships with others (family members, health care professionals, neighbors, friends, co-workers).

Most important, consider: What will your culture grow?

It's a Double Whammy: Delegate and then Dabble

You may be the best one in your family to provide care. You have the instinct, the fortitude, and sometimes, the stomach, that seems to elude other family members. You may be the best all-around caregiver, but others have skills that can be useful. Take advantage of other family members' skills by delegating some of your caregiving responsibilities.

For instance, your brother pays the bills and manages the finances; your sister makes phone calls on a regular basis to find out about community services that can help; your aunt pays for monthly respite services so you can take a break; your daughter does the grocery shopping and errand running every week.

When you delegate, you create more time for yourself. Then, use the extra time to dabble in activities you've always wondered if you would enjoy.

Think you have an artistic flare? Then dabble in painting your garden, drawing your caree's portrait, photographing snippets of your life.

Believe you can write the next Great American Novel? Then dabble in writing short stories, poetry, your caree's life story. Want to start your own business when your caregiving role ends? Then, dabble in brainstorming business ideas, researching how to start and run a business, talking to small business owners.

Delegating creates time to dabble, which expands your interests. Your dabbles will create a new self portrait; a self-portrait that's colorful, lively, and refreshed--a true reflection of you.

Caution

When the red flags appear, do you use caution?

The home health aide seems more preoccupied with your dog than in helping your mom. The doctor waves away your concerns about your caree's weight loss. The hospital discharge planner, while running down the hall, assures you he'll give you plenty of notice about your spouse's discharge date.

Out of the corner of your eye you can't help but see a red flag waving.

Your gut will tell raise those red flags. And, when it does, slow down, gather information, ask questions, determine the reality of the situation. Sometimes, you can change a red flag to a caution flag to a green flag. And, sometimes, you just have to drive away, knowing that another health care professional or resource is available to better meet your needs.

Garden

Our vegetable and flower gardens need our regular touch for watering, pruning and weeding. That combination of nurturing and eliminating keeps the garden healthy.

Our emotional gardens also need our on-going handiwork. On a regular basis, we can reflect on how well the individuals and relationships in our life work. Do they still support us? Do they honor us? Do they ensure we bloom? Do they accept our thorns?

If not, then weed. Weed what no longer works so you have room for new and better relationships to take and then to grow.

Today, what and who will you weed?

Outside

In the warm weather, it's wonderful to feel like outside is a wonderful alternative.

Often, it offers a welcome reprieve. You can go outside to take a walk, to sit in the backyard, to enjoy nature's blooms.

In a caregiving role, though, you can feel like you're often on the outside. You may feel on the outside of life--of activities, events, discussions, experiences. Caregiving can pull you so far in, that you can't see your way out.

Enjoy the outside knowing that you have the the inside tract on the secret of life. You know that life is about being there for those who need you. That life is meaningful when your actions match your values. That while others may choose to live only on the outside, you choose to live fully inside and out.

Go outside. You have what the world needs.

Inheritance

We think of inheritance as a sum of money given after death.

Inheritance is bigger, and more important, than that.

Every day, we have an opportunity to be on the giving and receiving side of an inheritance.

We receive an inheritance when we take time to listen to another's story. And, we really listen when park our story on the curb, which allows us to to focus on the story another tells us. When we listen with compassion and curiosity, we receive perspectives and insights, helping us to make stronger connections and a better relationship.

We give an inheritance when we take time to compliment a friend, to smile at a stranger, to enjoy another's presence. When we do this, we pass along good will.

So, today, what story will you inherit? And, what good will you leave?

Wave

I love the word "wave" because it has so many purposes. We wave hello and good-bye. The ocean greets land with its own wave of white foam. And, at sporting events, we coordinate timing of our arms and bodies in order to create a stadium-wide wave.

In caregiving, we also can wave. We can wave away a bad day, knowing that good days follow. We can wave "hello" to help knowing that involvement of others enhances the experience for ourselves and our carees. And, we can organize our journey so that we remain in sync with support and comfort.

And, when we wave "good-bye," we do so with a full heart, an enlightened soul and a belief in the future.

How do you wave?

Parade

Do you feel sometimes that you sit on a lawn chair as the parade of life passes you by?

You watch as the floats roll by: Retirement, Vacations, Carefree Days, Saturday Night Dates. The worst to watch, though, are the ones that seem to make up an easier life: Guilt-Free, Stress-Free, Worry-Free.

Rather than watching a parade that brings pain, choose to participate in a different kind of ceremony, one which reflects your place in life right now. Perhaps your celebration honors your values: Family, Responsibility, Sensitivity. And, perhaps the grand marshal of your parade is Purpose, because while you feel may life passes you by, you actually live life as it's meant to be lived--with meaning and conviction.

And, then, make plans right now to build the other floats--the ones which may have to wait a bit--for your parade to come.

Fireworks

It's Fireworks Season. We shoot off
fireworks as a symbol of our gratefulness for
living where we freely build a life for
ourselves and our family.

How can you set off your fireworks in honor
of all that you embrace?

You don't have to wait for dark to light your
sparklers. Your fireworks may be a glass of
lemonade with someone special at 3 p.m.
Or five-minutes of quiet at 8 a.m. Or a
thank you call to a special friend at 10 p.m.

The beautify of your fireworks is their blast
is felt, rather than heard. That kind of blast
can last a lifetime.

First

We welcome a first with every season's change.--a first day. What will be a first for you today?

Perhaps this will be the first day you consider your priorities and then put boundaries in place to protect those priorities.

Maybe this is the first day you decide that sadness and happiness can coincide within a day, that sadness does not exclude happiness.

Today may be the first day you decide a painful situation deserves a better outcome.

The wonder of our change in seasons is the beginning of a difference. So, how will today be your first day to be different?

Hot

This summer, how hot are you?

You heat up when you:

- do something just for you, even if that only involves five minutes of your time;
- enjoy a good laugh with a good friend;
- smile at those who love you and honor you.

And, you are hot because:

- you live a life of integrity;
- you treasure your special moments;
- you take the good with the bad, knowing one can't exist without the other.

You are hot!

Dip

Do you need a refreshing dip in the pool this week?

A dip in the pool refreshes, energizes, renews. A dip in the pool clears your head, presents a new solution, shows you the way.

No pool?

Take a dip by taking a nap when you need it, slowing down to catch your breath or enjoying quiet time with a refreshing glass of lemonade.

This week, take a dip.

Grow

A family caregiver, Donna, once told me that she only developed her green thumb after her caregiving journey began. Before caregiving, Donna's plants were brown and lifeless. During caregiving, her plants bloomed.

What have you grown since caregiving began for you?

Think:

- How have your skills and talents grown?
- How have your relationships grown
- How has your wisdom grown?

You are different--better--because of caregiving. You have grown. You are green, in the prime position to make the most of your life. Celebrate it.

Torch

It's sometimes hard to see your way, and so much about the caregiving experience seems to block your view (other family members, the health care system, your caree). Which decision is right? Which path at the fork in the road leads to the answers?

When you carry a torch, you often carry the power to your answers. Your torch can be the comfort your support group brings, the wisdom your best friend offers, the personal resolve you've gained over the years. Your torch illuminates, enlightens, guides.

It shows you the way.

Truth

You may look into your future and see….
More caregiving. It's hard to predict how
long your caregiving role will last; your
hunch, though, tells you it will last longer
than you expect.

How do you make it for the long haul?

Tell the truth.

Be honest about what you can do, what you
need help with, and how you are feeling. It
may be hard to be truthful, but the truth will
set you free (really!). Today, take an honest
look at your caregiving role. And, then tell
the truth: To your support group, your
caree's health care team, and most
important, yourself.

Your truth ensures that the caregiving
experience stays a positive one for you and
your caree.

Feel Good

You may wonder: How in the world can I feel good when so much badness (pain, worry, fear) surrounds me?

You will have bad moments, which may stretch into bad days, when you can't feel anything other than just bad. You will have good moments, though, when you feel peaceful, content, on purpose. When you have those good moments, allow them to become your good days.

Savor your good days; you've worked really hard to have them. They are yours; it's okay to keep them for yourself. And, your good days have a spill-over effect on everyone in your life.

Feel the bad days, then let them go. Embrace the good days, welcoming them to stay.

Bath

The aches of caregiving can seem to permeate your body: Your heart aches, your head aches, you bones ache.

Your spirit has the bath oils needed to soothe your aches. Your spirit's bath oils include your courage, your commitment, your kindness.

You have a very special spirit: It cares for others. Just as importantly, it can care for you. Run your bath tonight.

~ **Fall** ~

"Autumn carries more gold in its hand
than all the other seasons."
~ Jim Bishop

Own It

You're having a really bad day--because your caree is having a really, really, really bad day.

No matter where you look, you just seem to see red.

You didn't want it to happen, but it did: You lost your temper (really, really lost it) with your spouse (or friend or sibling). You can't yell at your caree, but your spouse... Well, that's an easy target even though it wasn't deserved.

On your next bad day, own how badly you feel without passing on your bad day to innocent parties (like others in your life). Write in your journal how angry you are, call a member of your support group and vent about your day, write an e-mail to your online support group.

If you pass on your bad day, you just make a bad day even worse. Owning your bad day, then finding a healthy way to vent about it, is a great way to turn your bad day around.

Acknowledge

An emotion may be lying under the surface, but the emotion may be so strong and so scary that you may fight to keep it below.

You worry that when it comes out, it may be too strong to control. It may be how angry you are at a family member, or how worried you are about your caree's health, or how frustrated you are about your lack of free time.

Acknowledge your emotion, your feeling. Give it a name and then find a place to put it (in your journal, your garden, your daily walks, in your support group).

Acknowledging, naming and putting your feelings in a safe place empowers you to control, rather than be controlled. When it's under the surface, it controls. When it's out, you control.

Acknowledge--whatever it is.

Abundance

It's hard to see your life as full--abundant--
when it seems that it's just full of problems,
one right after another. And, when you're
tired of facing problem after problem, it may
just seem easier to live in the problem.

Consider this:

When you focus on the problem, you live in
the problem. When you focus on the
solutions, you live in abundance.

You have abundance in your life, even in the
face of problems. Choose to embrace your
abundance as you pursue the solutions that
work best for you and your family.

One Step

You've got so much to do. And, it seems that everyone you know needs your attention. It can be paralyzing, thinking about all you do for your family.

When you feel overwhelmed or unsure or just defeated, just concentrate on taking one step. One step might be one phone call, one support group meeting, one physician appointment, one errand.

Just take one step; one step after another will keep you on the right path.

Persist

You face many battles as a family caregiver: Battles with the medical community to secure appropriate and timely treatments for your caree; battles with your family to receive the support you need; battles with community organizations to qualify for the assistance you deserve.

Phew! That's exhausting!

Take regular breaks from your battles, but persist in pursing positive outcomes for you and your caree. Your persistence will pay off.

Big

I had a friend who married a man who bragged about his big house. To him, a big house made him a big man.

In our society, my friend's husband isn't the only one who measures bigness by the size of material possessions. Because of your caregiving role, you may feel that you've sacrificed one material possession after another, perhaps to the extent that you feel you have very little. The savings account for the summer house by the lake paid for the ramp over the front stairs of the house. The long-planned European vacation is long forgotten as any extra money will pay for a future bathroom remodel. Your closet, once full of the latest fashions, holds only clothes of comfort--jeans, t-shirts, sweat pants.

Some may wonder how you live without the summer house, the European vacation, the latest fashions.

In truth, our heart and our courage make us big. Our bigness can be measured not by our big possessions but by our big acts.

Someone needed care. You stepped up to the plate. You took on a big responsibility.

What you're replaced with your caregiving role--by being an advocate, a caregiver, an inspiration--will always dwarf the largest mansion, the sleekest car, the grandest jewelry.

Because you care, you are big.

Difference

You may wonder, "Do I really make a difference?"

In particular, on those difficult days, when you don't hear "thank you", when you don't see progress, when you don't have help, it may be hard to see the difference you make.

Know it: You make a tremendous difference.

You make a difference in your caree's life, in your community, and, yes, in our world. Your actions show the importance of taking care and of taking on. Because of who you are and what you do, you add a sparkle and shine to our world. You bring goodness and kindness to a sometimes cold and unforgiving world.

You are the difference.

Sizzle

We all have a passion, something (or someone) that makes us sizzle.

What's your passion that gives you your sizzle?

You may feel that you've lost it in your caregiving world. Your sizzle may take a back seat to your responsibilities.

Some days, it's okay to move it to the front seat, even if for just a few minutes.

On a regular basis, find your passion, play your sizzle. Giving yourself time to let your sizzle show is one great way to take care.

Thanks!

It's 9:30 at night. You've just helped your caree to bed, which includes bathing, brushing, and battling. There's no time of the day you both dread more than bath time.

But, your day isn't over--not by a long shot. You still have to help your daughter with her homework assignment, finish making your grocery list for the week's meals, and call your sister to give her an update on your mom. And, your spouse had a bad day at work and wants to cry on your shoulder.

Wouldn't it be nice, you think, if someone, anyone, would say, "Thank you"?

Nothing can bring you down farther than feeling that your actions and efforts are futile. You may wonder: Would anyone notice if I didn't do all that I do?

Remember this: Although others may not express gratitude for all that you do, your efforts mean that others live in a safe, healthy, loving environment. We tend to dwell too much on what others think, believing that if they think and then express that what we do is okay, then we are doing okay.

You know that you make a tremendous difference in the lives of your family. Whether or not they tell you does not change this fact. You know it.

Star

When you look up to the sky at night, they take your breath away.

The stars, the wonder of the universe. They seem so small, but they throw such a glow, visible for thousands of miles.

Just as you admire the stars, the universe admires you, our world's star. You shine, you glow.

Look at you. You are a star.

Good Luck

Have you walked under a ladder? Has a black cat crossed your path? Did you break a mirror?

Or, did you merely get out of bed?

Do you sometimes feel you have lots of luck--it's just all bad?

The worst part about bad luck is our tendency to blame misfortune on ourselves-- as if we can produce it.

Bad luck isn't your creation. It's not you, it's just the ups and downs of life. Bad luck is nothing more than a series of unfortunate incidences. Give them greater significance and they become greater. Treat them as blips on your radar screen that you negotiate and you'll overcome.

You are wise and strong. You are bigger than any bit of bad luck. You are your own good luck.

Full

Do you end the day feeling empty?
You deserve to feel full at the end of the
day!

And, not just full from a good dinner.

You deserve to feel full with the knowledge
that you did good today, that you made a
difference, that you used your talents, that
your hard work was recognized and
appreciated. It would be nice to hear that at
each day's end, wouldn't it? Sometimes, the
people in your life end their days empty,
which makes it difficult to fill you.

So, know this:

- You did good today.
- You made a difference.
- You used your talents.
- Your hard work was recognized and
  appreciated.

Be full!

Open

When life becomes difficult, it may feel like a good time to stay closed. Your pain may feel so intense that it's too hard to share, so you keep it closed to friends and friends. It may just seem easier to keep the pain under lock and key.

This truly is the time to be open. Be open to opportunities to share your pain with just the right person; be open to times when you can disengage from the pain, even if for a few minutes; be open to the chances to move past the pain.

Be open. And, when you stay open, you stay open to receiving the love, support and healing you deserve.

Balance

You may feel like caregiving is a balancing act--balancing caregiving with relationships, work, hobbies, and rest.

You're also balancing your past, present and future.

For instance, does your past dictate how you act today? Meaning, because it didn't work then, do you believe it won't work now? Or, because you couldn't do it then, are you convinced that you can't do it now?

Do you worry so much about the future that you neglect the present? Do you focus so much on what could happen next week that you don't see the blessings you have today? Are you dreading what could happen next year so that you can't relax today?

It's good to bring lessons learned from the past into the present. And, it's important to take steps today to protect your (and your family's) future.

But, always live in the present. You have today, right now, this moment. How will you use it?

Story

What's your story?

Does your story reflect who you were, who you are, who you want to be? Or, does your story cement you in a past full of wrongs and pains, so much so that the listener loses focus of who you are today?

Tell a story about yourself that includes lessons learned (your past), your current goals (your present) and your dreams (your future). A story that includes your past, present and future respects who you were, who you are and who you will be. It also paints the complete picture of you.

What's your story? Start to tell your story in your journal.

First

Do you wonder how long you'll feel last
because your caregiving role seems to last
forever?

It's awful to feel last, that everything and
everyone good passes you by.

Know you are very first. You are first
because you were first to step in and help,
first to find solutions, first to advocate. Your
firsts will earn you a first-place finish.

You are a first. Your grace, wisdom and
kindness ensure you will never be last.

Sunset

Do you enjoy the sunset as much as the sunrise?

We might favor the sunrise because of the potential and possibility it offers. The sunrise means a start.

The sunset, though, offers views into Mother Nature at her best and, with it, closure. What a beautiful day when brilliant reds and orange end it for you.

Honor the sunset and sunrise. Beauty lies in beginnings and endings.

Passion

What trips your trigger? Who floats your boat? What sparkles your eye?

While caregiving can exhaust, sadden and overwhelm you, caregiving also can showcase your passion. It heightens who you are.

And you, you are spirited, creative and fun.

So, be those things in the activities, relationships and hobbies that play your passion. When your passion plays, you are who you are meant to be.

Beat

What benefits do you reap from your relationships?

You are a caring, nurturing, compassionate person. Because you know how to give, you may find yourself attracting takers. If you find yourself surrounded by takers, then take time to lose them. And, losing them is as simple as dancing away. When they ask you to dance, just dance away.

You deserve to have givers in your life--givers as good as you--who affirm, support and honor you.

When you have givers in your life, you can take turns giving and taking. The delicate dance of giving-and-taking is always right on beat when two hearts beat in unison.

Why?

Why me? Why my family? Why now?

When fate waves her hand and your life changes--and not, seemingly, for the better--it's natural to question fate's decisions to wave her hand in your direction. Why us?

Consider this response to fate's hand instead: Okay, it's us. How are we going to move forward?

The question, Why us?, cements you to one place. The question, How are we going to move forward?, unsticks you, putting you and your family in motion toward solutions, and more importantly, toward healing.

It's you. But, it's also up to you. How will you take a small step forward today?

Start

You may feel the end, the end of caregiving, will be difficult. You may dread the death (of your caree and of your role) because of the finality.

Because it ultimately, sadly, is about death, it's really, joyfully, about life. It's about living a good life. And, the good life you live after the death keeps your caree alive. Your caregiving makes it so.

It starts you and continues your caree.

Wind

Which way will you let the wind blow?

Will it blow north so that you face today and tomorrow, grateful for lessons learned, enthusiastic for new opportunities? Or, will it blow south so that you live in the past, fearful of what lies next and anxious about yesterday's wrongs?

Face north. You'll hit storms, but you'll see the stars and the rainbows. Face north, live for today while preparing for tomorrow.

Time

Everyone, it seems, wants a piece of your time.

How in the world will you have enough time for everyone? And, have time to achieve all you want in life?

Worrying about the lack of time can create a deficit--you may feel that you'll never have enough time.

Believe you have time. You have time for all that caregiving requires of you. You have time for all you want for yourself in life.

You have time.

Fairly Unfair

If you think long and hard enough, you'll
know precisely the moment it started.

Most likely, it started over a bike, a mitt or a
doll. Or, two of the three. Or, perhaps all
three.

You remember the unfairness of it all--how
one sibling got just what you wanted. And,
you? Well, you got the ugly flannel pajama
set. Or, the complete set of encyclopedias
about bugs.

The feeling of unfairness can follow you
through life, gaining speed during the
biggest and most unfair life test of all:
Caregiving.

In caregiving, fairness never seems to show
up. The unfairness began with the
diagnosis--it's almost unbelievably unfair
that anyone, much less your family member,
should receive the news that they have
cancer, or Alzheimer's, or diabetes. It's even
more unfair if the diagnosis is the result of
poor life choices completely out of your
control, but now very much a part of your
life. You didn't smoke, for instance, but your
lungs ache from not having enough time to
breath—really, really breath from relaxation
—as if you inhaled 20 Marlboros every day.

It's unfair how unhelpful and uncaring the
health care system can seem. It's beyond

unfair that you have to scrape and fight for any help. It's unimaginable how unfair it is that your efforts are often met by ungratefulness.

It's just unfair.

But, here's what's fair: The blessings and abundance you recoup for facing life's toughest battle with courage. And, it's truly fair that you can live life without regrets. Because you could, so you did.

The unfairness now will become your life's fair, a carnival of wisdom, peace and joy.

~ Winter ~

"Sometimes our fate resembles a fruit
tree in winter. Who would think that
those branches would turn green again
and blossom, but we hope it,
we know it."
~ Johann Wolfgang von Goethe

Home

You know you are home when you feel warm (even when it's cold), safe (no matter what's happening out in the world) and calm (although calamity may surround you).

Home is how you feel, not where you live.

Welcome home.

Reach Out

It's easy to reach out to friends when you feel good, when all is well, when you can smile without effort. It's nice to share good times with good friends.

It's hard to reach out when it's not going well, when tears come much easier than smiles. As hard as it may be, the most important time to reach out to friends is during those difficult times. And, when you reach out, tell your friends what you need, whether it be an empathetic ear, a good laugh, or assurances that all will be okay (it will!).

On a down day, call a friend. Ask for what you need. Your day will get brighter.

Wealth

You've made so many sacrifices to provide care: Your time, your relationships, your career, your pocketbook. It's hard not to wonder if these sacrifices are truly worth it?

When you make the right choice and stay on the right path (and you know best which is the right choice and the right path for you), you accumulate riches that are immeasurable. You gain a wealth that lasts a lifetime. And, such a wealth will some day replace all the sacrifices you've made.

Your wealth will be limitless.

Boundary

You may think: Because you are the only one who can, you must do it all.

Not true.

Boundaries are an important part of your caregiving experience. Boundaries dictate interactions with other family members; how long you can provide heavy-duty, hands-on care; how long you can manage between regular breaks. Boundaries help you maintain your own mental, physical and emotional health.

Without boundaries, you will do too much, for too long, for too many people. Without boundaries, you sacrifice yourself. With boundaries, you ensure respectful discussions, purposeful actions, well-deserved time to yourself.

When you respect your limits, you earn respect, from yourself and from others in your life.

What boundaries will you set today for your own well-being? And, how you will celebrate the boundaries you set?

Control

Ewwww… You'd like to have some control. So much in your life has been out of your control. You'd give anything for a little control:

1. Over a certain family member, who never keeps his word on when he'll stop to help.

2. Over the doctor, who seems to take two-week vacations every month, and can never call you back to answer your questions.

3. Over your caree, who seems unable to respect your schedule and your responsibilities.

Living with the thought that your life is out-of-control may make you just want to pull the sheets over your head and stay in bed forever. But, controlling everyone and everything can be exhausting.

You can't control your family members-- they must live with the results of their actions. You can't control the doctor--but you can find another one. You can't control your caree--but you can ensure that he has the medications, activities and community services that he needs.

You can only control yourself: Your actions, your words, your solutions.

As for the rest… Let Go and Let God.

Yesterday

Do you live in the mistakes of yesterday?

It's okay that something went wrong yesterday or last week or last year or last decade. We are imperfect beings, meant to live imperfect lives.

Mistakes of yesterday only become problems when they cloud our opportunities of today. Don't let yesterday's mistakes rob you of today's blessings.

Let go of yesterday. Live today.

Insight

At times, you may find your caree reacting
to the present as if he or she were still in the
past. The aging process may unleash
emotions and actions based on events that
occurred fifty, sixty, even seventy years ago.

To gain insight into your caree's past, take
time to review old photos with your caree.
Ask questions about your caree's first love,
first job and first heart-break. Reminisce
about past holidays, birthdays, anniversaries.
And, ask your caree about past historical
events.

When you help your caree review the
important events of his or her life, you gain
insight into your caree, painting a larger,
more colorful picture of him or her. And,
when you gain insight about your caree, you
gain insight about yourself. And, that insight
helps you paint your own portrait with
vibrant, life-affirming colors.

Escape

You'd love to escape--leave it all behind.
Forget your problems, your worries, your
anxious moments. But, how can you really
escape your life?

Taking a breather from an emotionally
exhausting experience, like caregiving, can
breathe new life into your life. A night out, a
weekend away, a week-long vacation are all
wonderful breaks. But, you can't always
physically get away, which is why regular
emotional get-aways are so important.

You take an emotional vacation, when you
find yourself engrossed:
--In a good book;
--In a tearjerker of a movie. (A good cry can
be a wonderful release. And, sometimes it's
easier to cry for someone else's life rather
than your own.);
--In a fabulous day dream in which you star.
(You are the toast of Manhattan because of
your well-paying, glamorous job; You have
won the lotto and now spend time at your
homes in Hawaii, the South of France and
San Francisco; You finally tell your helpless
family members what you really think of
them).

Even the briefest of escapes can transport
you, refresh you, remind you of a life
outside of caregiving. Be sure to plan, and
allow for, regular escapes. You deserve
them.

Romance

It's hard to imagine romance and caregiving sharing the same house. It would seem that one cancels out the other.

When love lives in your house, so does romance. And, when love lives in your heart, you know romance.

Enjoy!

Catch-Up

Are you playing catch-up? You might be playing with your bills, your job, your kids, your caree. Always try to stay even or even move a little ahead, but seemingly always running to catch up.

You may find that the more energy you put into playing catch-up, the more you find yourself playing. Life can become one long game of catch-up before you know it.

It's okay to never catch up.

This week, say "uncle" to catch-up. Throw in the towel. Wave the white flag. And, then enjoy the time you gain from not playing. Take time for yourself this week, even if for only five minutes.

Take it and embrace it.

Family

You grew up with them--the siblings. Or, you raise them--your adult children. But, now that caregiving has entered your life, they seem to be strangers. You wonder: Where did these insensitive, overbearing and selfish creatures come from? This is my family???

It's painful to learn that siblings and adult children can sometimes bring problems, rather than solutions, to the caregiving table. And, it's heart-breaking to discover that you really can't count on those you thought you could count on most.

The good news, though, is that a family can take many shapes and forms. And, caregiving will bring you a new family: Members of your support group; other family caregivers at the adult day center; the home health aide who dotes on your caree; the neighbors always willing to lend a hand. Good hearts make the best family members.

You are blessed with people in your life who love you. You are blessed with a great family.

Saint

Do you people call you a "saint" for all you do? Do they say, "You must be a saint"?

Being compared to a saint can bring with it lots of pressure. Those are big shoes to fill, especially because it's normal to have days that are full of un-saintlike thoughts, actions and words.

That's okay. More than a saint, you are a human.

And, being human means you are blessed with imperfections. You will have moments you would like to erase, words you would like to take back, thoughts you wish you could control. But, you also will have moments when you know just what to do, say words that offer amazing comforts, and experience thoughts that bring great peace.

You are human. And, your imperfections make you just perfect.

Fight

Oh, the fights! You may feel like you fight with your family members, with the health care providers, with the dratted folding wheelchair.

The worst fights, though, may be the ones you have with yourself.

The internal battles over what's best, what's right, and what's next can exhaust and sometimes paralyze. You may get so caught up in your internal war that you lose sight of your external wins--your caree is safe, has the care he or she needs, and has an advocate (you) to ensure the safety and care continue.

Today, make peace with yourself. You will have battles in caregiving. Just don't start a duel with yourself.

Down-In-The-Dumps

You'll have those days in which you'll feel Down-In-The-Dumps. And, on those days, family and friends may say, "Oh, it's not that bad. Come on, look on the bright side."

On those days, when you hear those remarks, it's okay to turn a deaf ear. Because it often is that bad and it often is impossible to look on the bright side. When you feel down, look for a support system that validates and empathizes, that shows they understand that you have a right to feel blue.

Sometimes, you can't help but feel Down-In-The-Dumps at times. It's okay to feel it.

Fun

A member of one of our online support groups once wrote:

"I dread the sameness of every day. Every day it's the same--personal care, meal preparation, a struggle here and there over the walker, the incontinence briefs, the medications. The sameness is just awful."

When it seems that your caregiving days become drudgery, look to add some fun. Play music during personal care time; take a drive, put in your favorite CD (or tape) and sing as loud as you both can; play your favorite dance music after dinner and cut up the dining room rug; rent your favorite comedy for a special Friday Night at the Movies in your own living room; reminisce about your favorite memories and photographs.

So much about your caregiving life can bring you down. And, that's why you and your caree deserve some fun every day.

Enjoy!

Dust

What needs dusting in your life? Your time alone? Your friendships? Your hope? Your travel bags?

This week, take time to dust. Make time for your needs, even if for just five minutes. Dust away the cobwebs by taking a nap, reading a good book, watching an engrossing movie, enjoying a quiet drive, calling a good friend.

You'll never know what you uncover when you dust.

Gut

You may feel that your true challenge in caregiving is making decisions. What's right for your caree? Whose opinion is right when it comes to a treatment decision for your caree? Which home health aide is right to take care of your caree? Which nursing home is right? What's right???

These decisions can weigh heavy on you. In times when you worry about making the right decision, listen to your gut--and then have the guts to follow that intuition. Your guts will let you know which decision is right (you'll feel at peace) and which isn't (your stomach rumbles will keep you awake at night).

You have the knowledge, the wisdom and the insight to make the right decisions on behalf of your caree. Your gut knows it!

Energy

We need it so much--a full tank of energy. Sometimes, the tank seems empty--you're out of energy.

When you're feeling lethargic, lazy or low, schedule time in your day to re-energize. Maintaining your energy level with ample time to rest is as important as doctor's appointments, healthy meals, and exercise. Let other tasks slide for the time being; they'll be there when your tank is full. And, you'll get more done when you give your tank time to refuel.

Resting is good. And, resting without any guilt is best.

Glory

It's hard to imagine that glory can be a part of your vocabulary. Where's the glory in incontinence care? In the five loads of laundry you do every day? In the white lies you tell you caree so, well, so she will?

But, in all you do for your caree, there is glory. And, you, in turn, are glorified in every caregiving duty. You honor, and are honored, by your ability to provide care during the most difficult and trying circumstances.

Your crowning glory? Your goodness, your compassion, your gracefulness.

Enlightened

You may feel, at time, disillusioned. Disillusioned that life has become this-- caregiving.

If you can, try to move from disillusioned to enlightened. When you make the move from believing that your life has become cursed to believing that life is full of gifts, you flip a light switch. You now see all the possibilities in life, rather than all the limits.

You have amazing, special and valuable gifts. And, because of your caregiving role, you have a unique opportunity to use these gifts. Be open to these opportunities. Live enlightened.

Heaven

How do define your heaven on earth?

Sometimes, caregiving can be described as, well, hell. Your family member is ill, sometimes critically so; your family is in crisis; you find yourself in a constant state of expecting the worst.

You've lived through hell. Now, how do you create your heaven on earth?

Spend some time this week daydreaming:

- About your next vacation
- About your next day off from caregiving
- About your best friend
- About your proudest accomplishment
- About your greatest gift
- About your most cherished blessing
- About your most amazing opportunity
- About your favorite memory
- About your wish for your future

You've just created your ingredients for heaven on earth! Mix, shake and pour.

You're in heaven!

Happiness

Are your happiness and your caregiving responsibilities mutually exclusive?

Caregiving can sometimes overwhelm you with sadness, grief, anxiety, depression. You will feel these emotions--that's a normal reaction to a very trying experience.

Make sure you leave room for happiness, as well.

You may think: How can I be happy when my caree has so many problems? Is it fair to be happy?

Yes! We all deserve happiness, particularly in times of deep concerns and worries. Happiness lies in your life's details: your relationships, your accomplishments, nature's beauty. Enjoy a joke, share a laugh, offer a smile.

As a caregiver, you have moments of despair. When the happy moments come, treasure them!

Heavy

Sometimes, it may seem too heavy to bear, this caregiving load. The worry, the loneliness, the exhaustion, the constant need to adjust, the pressure to make a decision on a dime.

This is a heavy load you carry; it's a load that requires the strength of many hands. Turn to help--from family, from friends, from support group members, from neighbors, from community agencies and social service providers. With the help of many hands you'll find that your load will lighten.

You've stepped in to help when a family member needed you. You deserve the same-- a load that you can carry with the help of loving hands.

Goals

Who do you want to be this year?

The true lesson in caregiving is that you only have control over yourself. With that in mind, who do you want to be this year? Do you want to be a writer? Painter? Gardner? Do you want to be assertive, unyielding, direct in your requests?

Take some time this week to daydream about who you want to be. Then, this year, be that person. It's all in your power.

Charge

This week, consider what needs your attention. In what parts of your life can you take charge?

Some much of you seems to go into caregiving, with little left for what and who you once enjoyed. Take charge and take some back--those relationships, interests, hobbies, loves you've put on hold. You may only be able to take back pieces; use those pieces to create something new, something that you've dreamed of creating.

Piece by piece, take charge.

Clutter

What clutters your life?

Clutter can affect our physical environment (disorganized closets, piles of un-filed paperwork, unopened mail) and our emotional well-being (negative, unhealthy relationships).

This week, take a look at how you live and who shares your life. Consider: What's the clutter? Then, take one small step to minimize the clutter.

When you chip away at the clutter, you create room in your life for abundance.

Best

In caregiving situations, you may have find
yourself thinking: How can I do this better?

Looking for a better way to provide care is a
wonderful idea. Better ways to provide care
improves your day--and your caree's. You
will find opportunities to improve
caregiving tasks, such as how to transfer
your caree from a wheelchair to a commode,
or how to prevent skin breakdown, or how
to make the drop-off at the day care center
easier for you and your caree.

But, when you it comes to you and how you
are doing, know this:

You are always doing your best. And, you
can never do better than that.

Now

As a family caregiver, you may find yourself pining for holidays past, when your caree was well and life seemed simple. You also may find yourself dreading the New Year, suspecting that you may not want what next year will bring.

To help you cope this holiday season, concentrate on the now--the good of today, the blessings of this holiday season. Live in each moment that you and your caree share.

Remember the past in order to comfort; look to the future in order to prepare. Live in the now to reap the joy of the season.

Review

This week, take time to review this past year. What worked well? What could have worked better? What areas in your life (responsibilities, relationships) would you like to change?

You may feel that this year was a year full of losses, disappointments and heartache. Think of those losses, disappointments and heartaches as opportunities for growth. This is hard to do, but if you can find some positives in the negatives, you can reap more positives than negatives in the coming year.

This year gave you nuggets of wisdom and lessons learned. How will you use these next year?

Believe

Your life has changed because of an illness or disability. Your life has changed so much it's shaken your faith. You find it hard to believe, because you can barely believe what your life has become.

An illness or disability robs you and your caree--of your self, your freedom, your security. But, don't let it take your belief.

Believe:

Believe in your abilities, in your successes, in your dreams. Believe. Your belief will take you exactly where you want to go.

Merry

During the holiday, we are told to Make Merry or Be Merry. We are wished a Merry Christmas.

Can we really have Merry in our life?

Yes. You actually already do. You have Merry when you hold your caree's hand, when you share a smile with a loved one, when you let peace live in your heart.

Merry is about transcending a caree's disease process, honoring what you love, and staying with forgiveness.

You have Merry. Pass it on.

Wonderful

Does "wonderful" describe your life?

Yes, it does!

It does because of you. You make it wonderful because you believe in yourself. Because you keep the faith in yourself, even on your rough days. Because your decisions reflect the respect you have for yourself, your family and your values. Because you know about the precious commodity called time--so you use your time wisely. Because you live fully in a world that turns on forgiveness, love and kindness.

You are your wonderful life.

About the Author

 Denise M. Brown, Professional Caregiving Coach and Speaker, began working with family caregivers in 1990. She was an early developer of online support groups for family caregivers, launching her first in 1996 through her website, Caregiving.com. Through her website, seminars, writings and coaching practice, Denise helps family caregivers and health care professionals find meaning in their caregiving journeys.

To reach Denise, please visit Caregiving.com.